T0365359

LIFE EXPLAINED IN POETRY

R. SWAMY

Print information available on the last page

Rev. date: 06/04/2018

To order additional copies of this book, contact:
Xlibris
0800-443-678
www.xlibris.co.nz
Orders@ Xlibris.co.nz

Life Explained in Poetry

INTRODUCTION

This book is a collection of some of the poems I've written since my early teenage years. They reflect the experiences I've had or things I observed over the years, and how they affect or make me feel.

The key topics focused on in the book are disability issues, inspiration, poverty, and love. The reason for this is because I've faced a lot of barriers throughout my life, but thanks to persistence, the love and support I received from my family and friends, and the difference God made in my life, I am still standing and have progressed one way or another over the years. To add to this, as I've aged, and observed the poverty millions suffer from, I realised how fortunate I've been regardless of these barriers.

I would like to dedicate this book to my family and church friends, who have helped my wife and I face the obstacles we faced in recent years. Most of all I would like to dedicate it to my late son, Mataru Taimerua, who passed away in year in February 2017 at a young age of 5 ½ years. Mataru was a persistent fighter who faced much tougher battles than I have due to his severe disabilities. Yet, his selflessness and the power of his love helped him throughout his life, and my wife and I will ALWAYS remember the difference he made in our lives and the impact he made on others too.

DISABILITY CHALLENGES

I have lived a life with various "ups" and "downs" as we ALL do. I was born with cerebral palsy and epilepsy, which not only created extra obstacles for me to face from the early years, but also created major challenges for my parents to tackle from the very beginning. Fortunately, unlike many parents, my mother was determined to enable me to live a normal life in the mainstream rather than one of segregation.

Therefore, though she was often questioned by her friends and relatives, my mother encouraged empowerment and independence, as much as possible, from the very beginning. Hence, I didn't even hear the word "handicapped" till my first day in primary school.

THE ONE AND ONLY ONE

R.Swamy (2nd Oct 2009)

How can I ever forget thoughts about a mother like mine?
How can I not remember the everlasting love I received from her since the day of my birth?
How can I even think of wiping out deep memories of my one and only mother?

A mother who has and always will love both her children pricelessly.
A mother who sacrificed her precious life and strong career for the better of her son.
A mother who created and retained deep-rooted hope that brought light into my dark life.

I will always love my mother from the bottom of my heart, as I have throughout life.
I will always pray for my mother's joy and well-being, and
I will NEVER lose the beloved memories of my one and only loving mother.

This poem expresses my love and gratitude for my mother who sacrificed her career for my upbringing and helped me overcome disability issues in childhood.

To this day I can remember how heart-broken I was to hear that word, and how I was initially upset with my mother for not revealing the "truth" to me. However, rather than give in to what I had heard, my mother then taught me that I was not handicapped, but simply disabled. Yes, I would face more challenges than other children did, but I did have my own strengths, and my beloved mother encouraged me to focus on my strengths rather than weaknesses. It was thanks to this attitude that I was able to overcome a lot of barriers I faced in childhood, youth, and adulthood.

THE JOURNEY OF LIFE

R.Swamy (July 21st 2008)

Carrying the burdens of life
He trudged on and on life's road.
A path which is the longest path he could ever dream of walking on.
A path which is rocky and hardly ever smooth.

Aim he simply did of climbing the mountain he faced.
That mountain which was too steep, too cold, and provided no shelter.
That mountain which many others had failed to climb,
...And were striving to be successful....

For only at the top would he be triumphant to overcome his burdens of life.
So climb he did,
Stumbling over his heavy footsteps.
Face he did harsh winds blowing against his face.
And fall he did over and over, with many pullbacks.

But he never gave up his hope.
That hope which remained as strong as ever,
No matter what he faced or what he suffered.

Thus, climb he did.
A climb that took long, tiring years, in which many fail.
And accomplish he did his goal of reaching the mountain's top,
And finally being triumphant of defeating his challenges.

I had written this poem when I had a breakthrough in my career and finally had a job that matched my University degrees of Master of International Business and Bachelor of Commerce, after doing other roles that didn't. Previously, I had faced years of discrimination and had been frustrated, but had continued to try with hope that one day I would overcome these problems one way or another.

As mentioned above, I do have epilepsy, a disability that can be very hard to deal with when your vocational goals are academic. The obstacles I faced throughout my life was having short-term memories due to the medication I was on, and having quite a few seizures per day or week in my youth when my seizures were not under control.

My Neurologist had also thought I wouldn't be able to do tertiary education considering my short-term memory issues and tiredness (side effects of the medications). Fortunately, I didn't listen to him as I was above average in High School and was able to overcome these issues by studying harder and making extra notes than others. To add to this, I have also learnt from this and carried it forth successfully into my vocational journey, and overcome barriers I ongoingly faced in the latter.

AWARENESS & ACCEPTANCE OF EPILEPSY

R.Swamy (August 30th 2004)

Everyone and not just one has at least a minor disability or another.

People live to be included in and not dissuaded from the community.

Independence is an issue everyone and not just a few struggle to gain.

Living in harmony with all and not few is a key requirement.

Ending the disharmony throughout the world is the foremost solution.

People holding hands and flying the same kite will struggle less.

Sunlight will arise and remain longer, with dark clouds fading away,

Yielding the deep value of humanity and acceptance.

I had written this poem whilst I was part of the Epilepsy Association and was encouraging awareness and inclusion for ALL. Whilst part of the Association I had tried to encourage some of the other members to get involved in more mainstream activities, because some had been brought up in more segregated environments. I also wanted to promote inclusion and help them gain confidence.

As mentioned earlier, thanks to my parents I had been brought up in mainstream. I didn't have any friends with disabilities till my adulthood whilst being in the Epilepsy Association and working in the disability sector as an Employment Consultant. This was not because I was avoiding fellow people with disabilities, but because I had not lived in segregation.

My wife also has cerebral palsy and was brought up in mainstream by her parents. She and I agree that it is very important people with disabilities are brought up in mainstream and included in the community as much as possible in-order to empower them.

THE SOURCE OF HELP & SUPPORT

R.Swamy (16th December 2005)

Each and every person is different.
No twos are same, regardless of similarities.
Each and every person has strengths AND weaknesses.
No person is perfect despite the person's strong strengths.

Each person has a door to open in life to enchant success.
No person is caged in a windowless room without a chance.
Each person has the one key responsibility to open the door.
No one's door can be fully opened by others but themselves.
Each person must open the door in-order to progress.
No person can be helped without helping him or herself.

Each and every person must discover his or her strengths.
No one is given strengths for they are learnt and developed.
Each person holds the key to a successful life journey.
No one should be locked out in a lockless room.
Each person must be supported to discover the road to success.
No person at all should be left behind.

This poem was written after I had started working in the Disability sector. Whilst working there and supporting people I learned that no one is perfect, and we ALL have opportunities to move ahead in life one way or another. To add to this, everyone needs to be supported one way or another to move ahead in life, but cannot if they are not willing to help themselves. Plus, there should be equity and inclusion in society.

Working in the disability sector at one point in my career was quite eye-opening. I had really enjoyed working for a Non-Government Organization (NGO) as an Employment Consultant for a few years. Whilst working there I had seen the difference some of these NGOs were making for people with disabilities in terms of overcoming segregation, discrimination, and promoting inclusion.

ITS PURPOSE & THE DIFFERENCE IT MAKES

R.Swamy (11ᵗʰ September 2006)

It is something priceless that not some but all need in life.
Something that emerges from the bottom of hearts that are strong.
All with the deep desire to brighten lives in ways that are sturdy and rife,
By rectifying assumptions and attitudes that are primarily wrong.

It helps many have more options and gain at least interdependence,
By replacing negligence in the community and building rapport,
Thus, bringing more satisfaction rather than repentance,
Which is the key that drives the principles of SOCIAL SUPPORT.

I had written this poem whilst working for a NGO in the disability sector. In this poem I was expressing how we ALL need social support in one way or another in our lives. Social support helps people gain at least interdependence, which is what such NGOs aim to accomplish and/ or maintain.

Despite my physical disability of having the left side of my body being paralysed due to cerebral palsy, I pursued various sports in mainstream from childhood. However, I had not explored golf till my early adulthood when my stepfather encouraged me. He assured I would not need two hands and shared how a friend of his, who was a regular golfer, was one-armed.

THE GOLFER

R.Swamy (April 13th 2004)

A golfer he is.
A golfer with many clubs.
A golfer who does not only make long shots,
A golfer who does not just putts, but
A golfer who makes the rights shots, and
A golfer who uses the right clubs at the right times.
A golfer who wins.

The poem is about my stepfather himself whose habits and attitude I have come to admire over the years. I admire the way approaches life and how his business has been successful.

Overall, it is not what sport a person plays that determines whether a person will win or not. It is how the person plays and the level of self-confidence the person has that determines the level of success.

I had lived in Manila, Philippines for most of my teenage years. It is while living there that I realized how fortunate I was compared to millions of people. Though I may have had disabilities my parents had provided everything I needed and desired from the very start. Living in Manila I literally saw what poverty was, and learned how I shouldn't self-pity myself due to my disabilities.

THE UNFORTUNATE & FORTUNATE

R.Swamy (26th June 1990)

Not everyone is fortunate.
Fortunate to have a good home and good source of food.
Many are homeless.
Many are foodless.

Not everyone is born in a home
With parents who worked hard and were successful,
Having not hesitated.

Not everyone is born in a home
In which there is no shortage,
In which parents devote their lives
For their family's welfare and happiness.

Though many are born
Having epilepsy or other impairments,
Fortunate they are to have no shortage,
And to have parents devoting their lives for their family's future,
Also supporting their children with the greatest care.

Many there are unfortunate,
And less there are fortunate, with lesser pullbacks than what the world faces.

I had written this poem in my teens, expressing the gratitude I had towards my parents for everything they had done for my brother and I, having worked hard throughout their lives. To add to this, I needed to be grateful for everything I had for though I may face challenges in terms of my disabilities it didn't compare at all to the poverty issues I observed most the people lived through in Manila.

INSPIRATIONS IN LIFE

Thoughts about progress and motivation to succeed have constantly passed my mind since childhood. Due to my disabilities and my mother's encouraging support for independence I often tried to run the extra mile and prove those who had the unconfident stereotype images of "handicapped" people incorrect.

Though I may not have always been successful at doing so, failures regularly deepened my determination. Repeated occasions did drive-up more depressing negative thoughts, but I never approve of giving up.

THE DOORS TO HIS DESTINY

R.Swamy (2nd July 2006)

*He had to open doors of an endless number
To discover what his destiny was in life.
Success hid behind certain locked doors, with keys lost.
Thus, he had to find these keys,
To overcome problems he faced and not be strained with gloom.*

*Over time he did open many good doors,
Solving the everlasting mazes he faced.
But he also passed through the wrong doors.
Yet he did not look back, for there was no path to the past.
Hence, learn from these mistakes he did for the better future.*

*As time passed his experience moulded with patience.
And, he solved the many mysteries he faced.
At long last he reached the final door,
That helped shut out his struggled past,
And opened the path to a brighter destiny.*

This poem is based on what my mother had taught me about life, and to this day reminds me of. When I had self-pity due to my disability during my childhood, she educated me that no one has a perfect life and that every person struggles somehow or other.

For everyone, once one goal is achieved another is created, and the latter are endless. Those who succeed learn from their mistakes so that these do not recur. Additionally, hope should be retained and not dispersed from the struggles faced in life. Thus, the key solution to life was solving problems, patiently learning from one's experience, and never giving up.

I didn't realise that I was going to face discrimination in the employment market even with a Master of International Business degree and above average marks till I graduated from University. It was then that I discovered how employers thought, and how I would face these discriminations for most of my career on an ongoing basis.

Thus, as mentioned previously, initially I didn't start my career in my desired field after graduating and first did telemarketing. However, I did appreciate working and held onto the hope that things would work out as I pressed on.

A MAN OF HONOUR

R.Swamy (29th August 2004)

Driven by his focused heart to thrive,

Incentive minded he is.

Given the privilege of being a very hard-working man.

Never shattered by the murkiness of failures that pass by.

Ignited by the strong determination to progress and not fall-back.

Testify the truth he does, despite the dark surrounding walls.

Yielded he has the tool to win against all, his own resilient dignity.

This poem was written while I was on an active job search whilst doing a fixed term two-year program for a government organization, which was coming to an end. I was getting quite frustrated, and wrote this poem to retain my DIGNITY and remind myself that things would work out regardless of what...as they did at the end of that year when I did get a permanent job elsewhere.

Despite the circumstances we may be in, we all struggle in life in one way or another. Therefore, it's important to remember to try and control our circumstances as much as possible rather than vice-versa. It's also always important to retain hope and NEVER give up, regardless of what.

THE CANDLE'S LIFE

R.Swamy (1st May 2001)

It was a candle,
A white candle.
And lit it was on
A dark night,
Where there was no light.

Light it produced.
Such light that
Killed the darkness.

Melt it did, slowly.
Producing no ashes that
Would stain its path.

Thus, as time passed,
The light edged away.
And, it was sunrise,
Which brought more light,
That the candle totally
Melted and died,
Having done its job.

This poem emphasizes how hope, like a candlelight, provides at least some light (if not a lot) to a person's life, especially during tough times. This hope helps the person survive till better times arrive and the circumstances change.

My parents separated in the late years of my teens, which was heart-breaking for me. Unfortunately, my younger brother had not experienced as much family life as I had, which was also quite upsetting.

FLOWERS IN LIFE

R.Swamy (20th June 2004)

Born it was like every plant,
A seed given birth by mother plant.
It took a long time for it to grow.
It did watch others bloom with flowers,
While it only had leaves.

But time did come when it too
Bloomed with flowers,
Bringing an aura of brightness to the plant,
In its own way.

Time came again when its flowers died,
And even leaves dropped.
But, it did regain its flowers over time.
Thus, time came and time went, again and again.

Observing nature's beauty has often brought about the thought in my mind of how the latter mirrors everyone's lives. Thus, a few times these thoughts turned into inspirational poems. The above and following two poems are good examples. The poems emphasise how each person eventually develops his or her own strength as they grow older and gain experience Thus, most go through struggles after times of joy, which often seem short-lived. Yet, similar to seasons, bad times do not last forever, but harmonious times may not return too quickly either. Overall, we need to keep strong and be prepared because life is like a period of seasons or a rollercoaster.

CLOUDED EXPERIENCE

R.Swamy (20th June 2004)

They are white clouds.
White clouds that cover the sky.
White clouds that promisingly colour the sky.
Bright clouds that lye relaxing on the sky.

Big, bright, and white as they are,
Time passes and times change.
Over time, relax less and burdened more they are,
Losing their white colour,
Being filled with darkness.

Thus, time and time again the clouds do cry,
Having been pushed down and impeded with trouble.
Yet, over time they are eased of their burdens,
And they do relax.
Nevertheless, time comes and times goes,
And neither ease nor pain lasts forever.

PATIENCE

R.Swamy (20th June 2004)

Born on a tree.
It is a fruit with a bright colour.
A fruit slowly ripening.
Beautifying the less colourful tree.
As time passes, the sweeter the fruit gets.

Then comes the time when the fruit is too sweet,
And falls down dead.
The tree is less colourful again.
Yet, as time passes
More fruits are born,
And bright colour is regained.

Each person's glory in life does depend heavily on themselves. Nonetheless, no matter how good a person may be, very, very few have lives that are problem free.

EACH PERSON'S STORY

R.Swamy 23rd September 2004)

Each person is an author,
Writing an autobiography each day and night.
Though no person knows what is to happen,
Though no person knows the end,
Think each person does of goals and morals,
And learn each person does from what is written.

Thus, write and read each person does at once,
And conclude each person does at the end of life,
Ending the story positively or negatively,
Depending on how each person writes.

In this poem I was trying to express how we do have control of our own lives. Though I've been really, really frustrated in life a lot of times, considering the issues I've faced, I've reminded myself there are people worse off. Plus, I have always believed in the value of persistence and how it works in life. Overall, though we may not know what will happen in the future we can try doing our very best and keep learning regardless of what.

One man I have admired throughout my life is my father. Though things may have got a bit tough when my parents separated, throughout my life I've been inspired by his background and his high achievements in life. In fact, it was his profession as an Economist that initially stimulated me to do my Masters as I wanted to follow his footsteps in terms of my career.

A SUCCESSFUL MAN

R.Swamy (16th December 2016)

Born in a family with low income.
Excuses were not made.
He prudently spent all his time.
He studied hard over time.
Using wisely all he had.

Not wasting the little money in possession,
He supported family as much as possible.
Working hard day and night.
Having bad light, without hesitation,
Studies were under streetlight.

He attained opportunities with confidence.
Earning good money with a good job.
And, a good name time and time again.

Thus, he remains standing
At a high position.
Still working hard,
With no reason to stop.

My father did grow up in a poor family. But, rather than make excuses as many do, he studied hard and made very good use of his time, literally studying under streetlights and saving money as much as possible. Thus, he earned scholarships thanks to his efforts and has had a very successful executive career. Thanks to this, he outweighed his background and lived his dreams, which reflects how efforts may pay out most times.

Though I mentioned previously I have lived a life that has been quite challenging in terms of study and work, one thing I haven't mentioned yet is that my wife and I adopted child, Mataru, who had very high needs (quadriplegic cerebral palsy, who had hearing impairments, was tube fed unable to speak, and was a wheel chair user). We had Mataru since 2012 and he needed a liver transplant.

Yet, though he did get his liver transplant in 2014, Mataru ended up with lymphoma cancer in 2015 and nearly died. Despite surviving ALL this, he unfortunately passed away unexpectedly this year in early February 2017. Having this son, who was our only child, reminded me how important it was to be grateful for everything good we have in life. The reason for this is because Mataru practically lived most of his life in the children's hospital, and couldn't express the deep pains he encountered (dystonia). But, regardless of this, most of the time he retained a strong smile, loved by many people, and was known as the "Smiling Man"! Mataru made a great impact on many people's lives throughout his life due to his persistence…

THE STRONG FIGHTER WITHIN

R.Swamy (13ᵗʰ July 2015)

His eyes tell his story.
Filled with love and affection,
He will communicate through his eyes.
Engaging lovingly to you endlessly,
The strong fighter within him is reflected through his eyes.
The fighter that will win ALL the battles he fights, regardless of his circumstances,
For he has Christ within him ALWAYS.

I had written this poem when our son was suffering from cancer. It was to express what a strong, loving boy he was. And, this was on an ongoing basis, regardless of his hard circumstances. He set a good example for others to follow.

I was born a Hindu and my childhood was as one. However, when I saw the poverty in the Philippines in my teens I turned my back on God blaming Him for it and not admitting that it has been mankind who has caused poverty through the centuries. Thus, I became an atheist at that point. Fortunately, in my late twenties I did discover Christ through my wife and eventually did accept Him as my Saviour as my questions were answered over the weeks/months at church. To be honest, it was as my faith grew that I did have more breakthroughs in my life, and felt much stronger inside as NEVER before, though things remain continuously challenging to this day.

HOLDING HIS HAND

R.Swamy (22nd September 2006)

I walked life endlessly for nearly three decades.
Blinded and lost I was on what to do or where to go.
Stumble I did time after time on life's road,
For my hand was not held, nor I guided by my father.

In time God came into my life.
At last I attained vision on where I am and where to go.
Listening to and following His words,
I now know what paths to pursue.

There are many challenges I face today and will face tomorrow.
Struggle I may, but stumble I won't,
For now the father of all
Holds my hand and guides me through it all.

Since I discovered Christ in life, I've felt much stronger spiritually. Because God works through people, at times of struggle I have been getting more support from people than previously. And, I also have clearer direction in life. Plus, I also admire how our church works as a team rather than individuals to tackle problems such as poverty in various locations locally and internationally, including the Philippines. In recent years it built an orphanage there and has other projects planned. In fact, this was an answer to one of my prayers considering what had pulled me away from Him in my teens.

R. Swamy

One of my favourite hobbies to-date has been doing jigsaws. These have mainly been "Wasgijs", in which you don't see the final picture, and photomosaic, in which the jigsaw picture is made up of small pictures. I have found these kinds of puzzles more challenging and a good way of getting my mind off work.

PUZZLES TO SOLVE

R.Swamy (14 October 2015)

Over time solve many jigsaw puzzles he did.
Some of small number, others of large.
Some he found easy, others hard.
All concerning the bigger picture,
And not the number of puzzles.
Yet, solve all he did,
Though struggle time and time again he did.
Each and every time
He was triumphant in the end.

As explained earlier, in 2015, our son attained lymphoma cancer and nearly died then which was heartbreaking. I wrote this poem trying to express how we ALL face various problems in life, which are like jigsaw puzzles. Some may be easy to solve, whilst other issues are complex, hard and frustrating. Overall, these issues link up to the bigger picture of life. Yet, through persistence, regardless of how many battles there are to face victory will be won.

Often life can be frustrating for people, and we may not understand what is going on and/or why certain things are happening to us. Due to these kind frustrations and pullbacks people can get too carried away at times.

IS LIFE A GAME?

R.Swamy 23rd December 2006)

Life is more than just a game.
Losing may stain your name.
It may cause a fierce fire in your heart to flame.
Covering your mind in shame,
And there is no one else to blame.

But, winning must be your aim,
For it helps you more than not being lame.
It brings you more than just fame.
Yet, careful you must be all the same.

In this poem I was trying to express that though life can be very hard for many of us at times, we do have control of our actions. We can overcome our obstacles in life, for it does bring a satisfaction to our hearts and minds. Nonetheless, we do need to be careful because sometimes we get too carried away in these things and overlook our other essentials which may backfire later in life.

One of my favourite hobbies from childhood till my late University years was playing chess. Over these years I learned the importance of strategic planning. As many of us know, it is very important to look several moves ahead to win chess games, which often isn't easy.

THE EVERLASTING CHESS GAME

R.Swamy (1ˢᵗ November 2008)

A chess game he plays.
Each move making a difference.
Think twice, move once he must.
If not, his opponent gains and slays.

Learn from successes and mistakes he must.
Only thinking of attacking and not defending
Causes failure on each move's test.
Thinking long term, and not only of one move,
Accumulates more hope to be the best.

In order to win the tournament, and not just a game,
Retain his skills and uncover more with experience he must.
If so, the tournament will end with him at last earning the fame

From my point of view, life has been everlasting chess game, as it is for all of us in one way or another. It is important to plan in terms of budgeting for holidays, family planning, house purchasing, retirement etc, and not just think about today. If these sort of things are not considered at least, life can be harder than otherwise.

I've grown up with one sibling, a brother, who is nine years younger than me. Fortunately, he has no disabilities and when he was born I had the vision that he would be my "left-hand" and enjoy life more and be more successful than me. Nonetheless, it also made push forward toward my goals and have more hope in life. Plus, as I had mentioned earlier, thanks to my parents' separation things had been harder for my brother, reflecting that disability issues sometimes aren't as bad as they look.

THE RACE OF THREE

R.Swamy (June 26 1993)

He cannot ride a bicycle.
He cannot drive a car.
He travels on foot all the time.

Though he cannot run as fast,
Though he cannot race the two,
Though he may limp a lot,
He runs, never giving up.

Though he is slower,
Though he struggles more,
He reaches his goal on time,
And is more satisfied having achieved more.

I wrote this poem a long time ago trying to express that though I was/am not as skilled physically or academically as my father and brother I wasn't going to give up, regardless of what. I know that though it will be harder to achieve things and people may generally doubt me, I will reach my goal and feel the satisfaction of doing so. The key thing is to believe in yourself rather than being doubtful.

To be honest, despite having breakthroughs in my career in the past, I've still struggled in terms of meeting the expectations of the employers, and balancing work and family challenges (our son's high needs). What this reflects is that life is hard for most people.

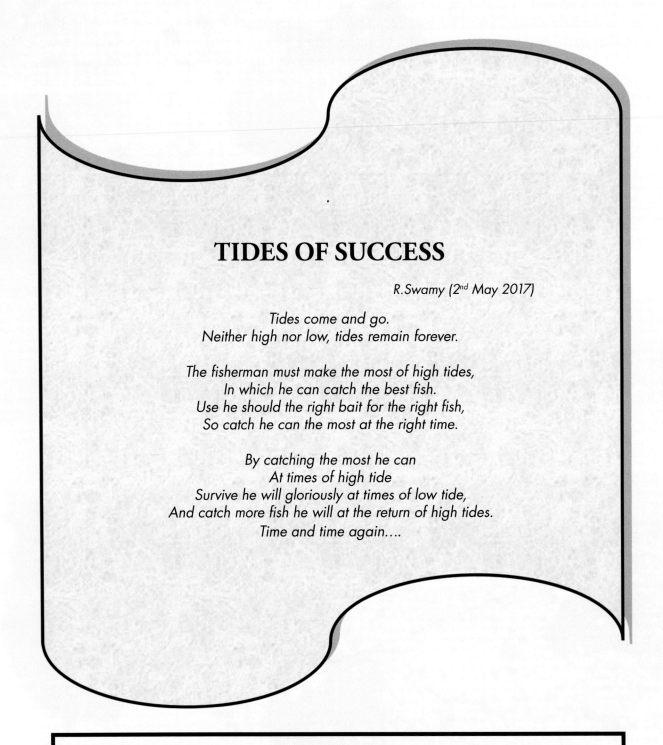

TIDES OF SUCCESS

R.Swamy (2nd May 2017)

Tides come and go.
Neither high nor low, tides remain forever.

The fisherman must make the most of high tides,
In which he can catch the best fish.
Use he should the right bait for the right fish,
So catch he can the most at the right time.

By catching the most he can
At times of high tide
Survive he will gloriously at times of low tide,
And catch more fish he will at the return of high tides.
Time and time again....

I was trying to express how life has seasons in this poem. It's important that we make the most of good times utilizing whatever we have available to prepare for the hard times. If we do so and learn from our past, we will be more progressive going forward.

In recent years, since we adopted our child, life has been more challenging and frustrating in terms of qualifying for jobs and overcoming my short-term memory issues due to the new medications I take. Yet, thanks the encouragement I've received from family and friends from church, I've been able overcome most of these issues and have a "Never Giving Up" attitude.

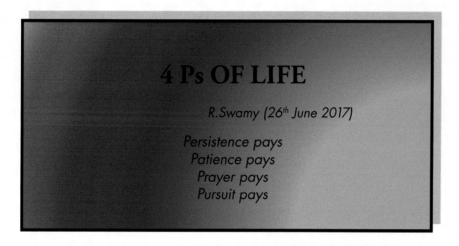

4 Ps OF LIFE

R.Swamy (26ᵗʰ June 2017)

Persistence pays
Patience pays
Prayer pays
Pursuit pays

In this poem, I'm trying to express that regardless of our circumstances, through strong persistence, patience, faith in God and pursuit of our goal(s), one way or another we will accomplish these goal(s). What needs to be understood is that it won't be overnight, and won't be on our own.

POVERTY IN THE WORLD

Having spent my youth and teenage years in countries such as Fiji and the Philippines, I did come to realise how fortunate I am regardless of my disability and family issues. The reason for this is because I had seen with my own eyes how people literally lived on a rubbish dump (in the Philippines – Smokey Mountain in the late 1980s), without any government support as they have in Organisation for Economic Co-operation and Development (OECD) countries. That memory will never fade…

LYING BY THE MUDDY OLD SHACK

R.Swamy (10th October 1988)

Lying by the muddy old shack.
His head throbbing with pain.
Mud covering his body.
His heart beating in vain.

Having a short life, of which no one cares,
It leads down, down, down,
To a place on earth where no one shares.
Nor gives a thing, not even a drop of water.

This was one of the first poems I had written in my early Intermediate School years. It was describing a picture I had seen in a magazine. Back then it was heartbreaking to see that the world's billionaires weren't taking many actions to help the poverty-stricken people from what I could see. Fortunately, times have changed and people like Bill Gates and Warren Buffet are now donating a lot of their time and money towards these issues. Plus, these people are encouraging other billionaires not to wait till their later years to consider such projects as they had.

What was and is very upsetting is that poverty factors are very extreme in these developing countries. Unlike in OECD ones you hardly see any middle ground. Plus, such poverty-stricken people are truly homeless, with very, very little food, and have very little choice in terms of where they can reside etc, because they are not given options as many are in OECD countries. I say so because I have lived in both such countries, and the poor people in OECD countries don't realise the power of the benefits they receive from the governments compared to those in developing countries who most often don't receive anything close to it. It's only later when a few of these people go to the developing countries that their eyes are opened, and they acknowledge through comments on news articles or Facebook that they weren't exactly "poverty-stricken" earlier in life as they had once thought. Due to the lack of appreciation and proper use of the support provided, child poverty has increased in OECD countries.

THE BEE & FLY

R.Swamy (20th June 2016)

One born in an environment,
Clean with a good source of food.
The other born in an environment,
Filthy, with only sources of leftovers.

One rich, with no shortages.
The other poor, striving of hunger.

One flying, being surrounded by wealth.
The other flying, being covered with dirt.

The rich living a life hardly experiencing shortage problems.
The poor living a life mainly experiencing problems.

I was trying to reflect how it's either black or white, with NO grey involved unfortunately, in terms of money in many developing countries. I.e. The rich are too rich and the poor too poor, which was heartbreaking to witness in my youth.

27

Back in the Philippines, daily I had seen a large number of people who were homeless and deprived of food without any options in life, as mentioned previously. To add to this, many of these were carrying a lot of family responsibilities on their shoulders which made things worse for them. Yet, I admired how they were hard working people, doing the best they could, with whatever resources they had available, and NEVER giving up.

THE LONELY LADY

R.Swamy (26th June 1991)

A woman who lost her age,
Throughout her time,
Stands still, all alone.

Feeble as she is,
Fall not she does.
Supported only by a stick,
Not so strong itself.

And feeble as she is,
Carry a loathsome burden she does.
Not asking for help,
Having not offered any.

Thus, walk on she will,
Because lose hope she does not.
And walk on she will,
Though helpless.

In the poem above and the following two poems I was trying express the hardships I had seen these people suffer ongoingly in the Philippines. The pollution made things worse for the people.

To add to this, due to the corruption and economy in these countries, many of these people didn't get the financial support they required. But, as I mentioned above, the victims did try doing whatever jobs they could, which reflects we should be grateful for EVERYTHING we have in our current circumstances knowing there are others in need...

LYING DEAD

R.Swamy (20th December 1989)

He lies on the road.
The dirty road.
Striving for food,
Suffering of hunger.

He lies on the road,
With no food to eat,
Nor given any food to eat.

He lies on the road,
Only drinking dirty water,
And breathing thick air.

He lies on the road,
With no hope to live,
Nor given any hope to live.

POVERTY

R.Swamy (16th July 1990)

Poverty-stricken they are.
Overrun by misery.
Virtually dying day by day.
Experiencing nothing but pain.
Raising neither money nor hope.
Tumbling down the roads.
Yet hardly given a hand.

As I was saddened by the poverty that I had seen with my own eyes in the Philippines and read about in countries such as India and Africa, which were shocking, I realised that it was no use simply watching. Thus, I took part in charity projects that my school organised to at least help in some way or other. Later, I also engaged in projects our church organises to help people in need.

THE BLOOM

R.Swamy (1st June 2001)

*The bright flower
Blooms with a lovely colour.
And is surrounded by others,
Blooming with different colours,
Colouring the air with a great variety.*

*And the bright flower
Does not stand alone,
With a sad face,
Surrounded by dull soil,
With no hope to be.
Surrounded it is by more flowers
To colour the air more beautifully.*

In this poem, I was trying to express how working together and selflessly in communities can be brighter. Plus, with good teamwork and support for one and other, no one should feel as though they are on their own and lose hope.

As I mentioned previously, later in life when I became a Christian I did realise and accept that it isn't God's fault there is poverty in this world (wherever), but due to mankind's greed and selfishness over the centuries. Nonetheless, rather than blaming Him, I concluded it was better to do the most we could on countering poverty in our everyday lives by trusting Him and donating to NGOs that focused on such missions, and serving at church as much as possible. To be honest, this was another reason I was keen to foster/adopt when we couldn't have our child, because I felt it would help counter the local child poverty issues I saw in New Zealand, whilst fulfilling our family desires.

THE ONE SOURCE OF LIGHT

R.Swamy 23rd September 2008)

This world is like an enormous room.
A room filled with darkness.
This world is surrounded with the thickness of gloom,
With most people "blinded" by the words and ways of doubt and disbelief.

Yet, it is in this room that God's true believers are also present.
Brightly enlightened by His strong words and ways.
It is on these committed believers that God shines His light.
An everlasting light that outshines all the darkness around it and simply stays.

It is the brightest light ever seen by any.
It is the light that over time will reach every corner of the room,
And wash off the surrounding darkness that may have lasted through time.
Replacing doubts and disbelief with strong faith and commitment that will bloom.

In the poem above and the following two, II was trying to express how we need to trust God through His words and fulfill the purposes we all have in life through our will and freedom, rather than blame Him for the issues around the world. This way, things will get better over time. And, this will be done by working together.

HIS WORDS & HIS WAYS

R.Swamy 22nd September 2008)

God brightens our paths each and everyday.
His words of wisdom guide us in the right way.
He also provides the freedom for us to do as we may.
Thus, with true will we should do what he wants and not fray.
This way the blossoms he spreads all around will always stay.
And no one should betray Him or go astray.

OUR CREATOR, THE MIGHTIEST WELDER

R.Swamy 7th April 2008)

He created the world and everything in it.
Welded us, people, to reflect Him in our lives.
Fitted us where we are to carry out our purposes for Him, and
Empowered us to engage in battle against the Devil, because…

We are His strongly moulded instruments.
Filled with His wisdom and faith in His mighty abilities.
Developed to effectively commit to His kingdom, and
Armoured by His blessings to completely defeat the Devil.

LOVE IN LIFE

I grew up being very close to Nani (grandmother), my mother's Auntie, who not only had played a big part in my young years, but also had brought up my mother because my mother's mother had died when she was a very young child.

IN MEMORY OF NANI-MY GRANDMOTHER

R.Swamy (5th September 1993)

Born I was with two mothers.
One of whom has died.
Nevertheless, her spirit will live forever and ever,
Lasting in our hearts and minds.

Never will we forget
Her love and care for one and all.
Never will we not remember
How others came first in her mind.

And pray we do that
She will live happily
In God's warm home,
And not suffer the pain
She experienced all her life and died.

I was trying to express my grandmother's love and devotion for us ALL throughout her life and how we will never forget her going forward. She had suffered from arthritis and asthma and one benefit of her death was that in heaven she was not going to suffer from these anymore.

I will always remember the strong, endless love my wife and I experienced through Mataru, our son, who passed away early this year. He made a big difference in our lives. We both admired how he countered the problems he faced due to his disabilities with love, and the strength of his selflessness – Never giving up.

OUR AMAZING MATARU

R.Swamy (10th November 2017)

Memories will remain forever of how he was continuously surrounded by an aura of love.
Although he experienced dramatic complexities throughout his life, he was a
Tough solider; born a fighter who never gave up, and countered pain with love.
And, despite his very high needs and complexities, he
Resiliently maintained a strong, selfless smile for everyone.
Unbelievingly facing the storms buoyantly, and touching the hearts of many people.

THE ROUND WORLD

R.Swamy (20th December 2012)

Stop being a clown.
Daddy is around, and
The world is still round.

In the first poem, I am trying to express how our memories of Mataru will always remain strong, and admiring how strong his selflessness was and the impact he made on many people's lives. I used to sing the second one to Mataru to entertain him. It still remains in my mind and brings back thoughts of spending time with him.

As detailed earlier, I have one blood brother, and our parents separated when he was quite young. In our early years, I had always hoped our father and us would work together as a team regardless of our parent's separation. Unfortunately, this didn't work out because our father travelled a lot in terms of his job and remarried and had another child later. Therefore, my brother and I haven't had a very close relationship with our father as I had hoped for in my young years. Nonetheless, I do love him, for he is our one and only father, and has taken good care of us both therwise.

THE TEAM OF THREE

R.Swamy (6th August 1998)

The sun, moon, and star
Play a vital role in brightening the Earth.
The Earth, our love.

The sun, our father, brightens the Earth's day.
Without the sun the Earth would have no warmth.
And without warmth the Earth is as good as dead.

The moon and star, his sons, bring light for the Earth at night.
Shining its path with twinkling light.
And without light the Earth would have no path to follow.

Thus, each member of the three is as important as the others,
For the Earth unites the talent of the three.
Working in a group of three helps the Earth's path
Brighten night and day,
And not be dull during the day, or gloomy at night.

I was trying to express how I had hoped that my father, brother and I would work together and be successful in running our home by combining our strengths. At this this point I also had the vision that going forward we would be able to run a business by combining our strengths. Unfortunately, none of this has taken place.

As I stated at the beginning of Disability Challenges, my mother did a lot me in my childhood and helped me overcome disability issues. Plus, I witnessed marital issues she encountered during my early years and tried my best to protect her as much as possible whenever needed. Due to this, our relationship also become like siblings in some ways over the years.

MEMORIES OF MOTHER & SON

R.Swamy 3rd October 2000)

Memories never die.
Everlasting in their minds,
Magnificently reminding them of old times.
Overcoming macabre burdens off their souls.
Reconditioning times of their woe, and
Yielding the tie between the two.

THE TWO'S RELATIONSHIP

R.Swamy 5th October 2000)

It is a relationship,
Which has been close since birth.
A relationship which has remained close for years.

It is a relationship which, when distant, is not a relationship at all.
It is a relationship, which will not be distant at all.
A relationship of a mother and son.

In these two poems I was trying to express how memories of each other will never die between my mother and I, regardless of what she and I encounter, or how hard things may get between us in terms of feuds etc. Our bond as mother and son will remain. I will always love and care for you Amma.

In terms of my disability issues, I am fortunate to have the parents, late grandmother, and brother that I do. Was it not for them, I'm certain my childhood would have been much harder as I've seen it is for people growing up with similar disabilities, unfortunately.

LIFE'S FOOT

R.Swamy 28th June 1992)

Born I was with one foot,
The other footless.

Had it been what was expected,
I would have stumbled,
Falling down to the dumps right after birth.

...But No....

It was they who were my other foot.
It was they who supported my life's body,
To walk straight on my fate's path.

It was they who helped me
Fall less and climb higher through progress.
It was they who gave my heart
Strength to live a life.
It was my Family.

I had written this poem during my teens when I was performing well in High School and had also received High Honour Awards etc. I was expressing how my family had the right attitude from the very beginning and helped me overcome the barriers I faced in order to empower me. What I observed in life is that the parents/families of disabled children often don't do so though they can, giving up on helping the children develop at least interdependence. What is overlooked is where will the children go once the parents die?

I met my wife, Janet, around twelve years ago in mid – 2005. It was our background of being from Fiji and the Cook Islands, and values of contributing to disability awareness that brought us together. Hence, I started writing poems to express my feeling about her and us as a couple. The following poems describe my love for Janet and the positive difference she has made in my life.

THE LOVING HONEY BUNNY

R.Swamy 12th September 2005)

She is a lovingly cuddly bunny,
Who is full of the world's sweetest honey,
And is also so hilariously funny.
She also does not have the faintest greed for selfish money,
And makes each and every one of my days so bright and "sunny"!

I had written this poem in the early stages of our relationship. In it I was trying to express how funny, warm, and selflessly caring Janet is, and how I love her company. To this day, this has been one of my favorite poems about her.

HER PRICELESS DIAMONDS

R.Swamy 22nd June 2006)

Each and every time I look at her lovely face,
Her bright green diamonds glimmer out in splendour, and
Their sparkling beauties elegantly shine out in glamour.

I may see them often, time after time, but
What glows out most from the depth is the value of
Her priceless love and affection,
All mirrored in her gorgeous eyes.

In this poem I was expressing how I love the beauty of Janet's eyes, which actually were one of the things that first attracted me to her. To add to this, I also voiced how her eyes reflect the love and affection she has for many people, which I've admired from our early days.

"TRUE" LOVE IN MY LIFE

R.Swamy 13ᵗʰ February 2006)

Janet is the one and only deep love in my life.
As she is the beauty I dreamt of in early days.
I hope that someday soon she will be my wife,
For true love, in the end, always pays.

As no other woman will ever replace her in my heart.
God bless us as a couple is what I plea,
With our relationship strongly bonded, never falling apart,
For true love is simply a purely endless sea…

In this poem I was vocalizing my love for Janet, and how I desired her to be my wife. Looking back, I can see how this poem does reflect my love for her, because though her had separated for a few months in 2016, Janet and I did reconcile before the end of the year. Thanks to our love for one and other, I know no other woman will be able to replace Janet in my heart, and always pray that we will stay together regardless of what we face.

THE STRENGTH OF THE TWO'S HEART

R.Swamy 18ᵗʰ March 2009)

Each person is born with half and not the whole.
She has one side and he the other.
Alone each side is unprotected like a thin glass,
Which could easily crack and be shattered to pieces.

Put together, a strong heart is born.
A heart that is well shielded against heart-breaking forces.
Once together the bright, warm sun does rise in the air of their lives.
And the heart remains together forever, in an endless sea of love and commitment.

I had written this poem to express how I felt that Janet and I were destined to be together, and that being together as a couple made both of us stronger. Furthermore, I was trying to vocalize the importance of love and commitment for one and other, as it is for all couples to be successful.

MY ONE & ONLY WIFE

R.Swamy 20ᵗʰ November 2014)

*You are the Angel of my life
The best gift I have or will ever receive from God.*

*You blossom with the strongest love and compassion for everyone around you,
Selflessly caring for us all.*

*You really are a true blessing from God,
With an inner beauty that outshines all darkness around us.*

*You are the one and only love of my life,
And everything I have ever prayed and dreamt of within.*

I had written this poem to express my love for Janet, and my admiration for her love and compassion for us all. It was during a period when our son was often being hospitalized, yet Janet remained very strong and supported him excellently, which many people have admired to this day.

Printed in the United States
By Bookmasters